JOHNNY CASH *for* UKULELE

Cover photo: Jan Persson/Redferns/Getty Images

ISBN 978-1-4803-8443-9

HAL•LEONARD®
CORPORATION
7777 W. BLUEMOUND RD. P.O. BOX 13819 MILWAUKEE, WI 53213

Visit Hal Leonard Online at
www.halleonard.com

All Over Again

Words and Music by John R. Cash

First note

Verse
Moderately bright, in 2

Ev-'ry time I look at you I fall in love

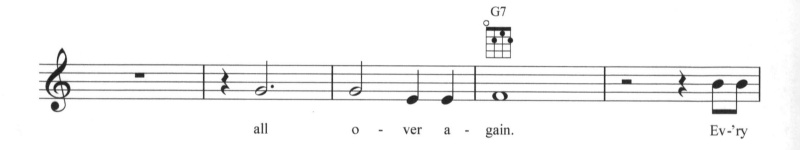

all o - ver a - gain. Ev-'ry

time I think of you it all be - gins all

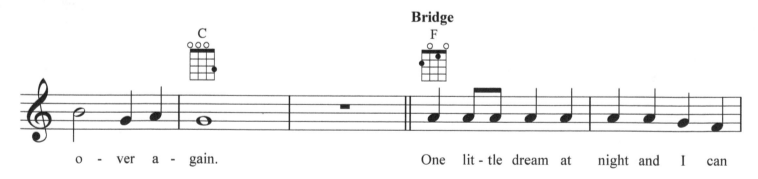

o - ver a - gain. One lit - tle dream at night and I can

dream all day. It on - ly takes a mem - o - ry to thrill me.

One lit - tle kiss from you and I just fly a -

way. Pour me out your love un - til you fill me.

Outro

I want to fall in love be - gin - ning from the

start all o - ver a - gain.

Show me how you stole a - way my heart all

o - ver a - gain. Ev - 'ry gain. ____

5

Big River

Words and Music by John R. Cash

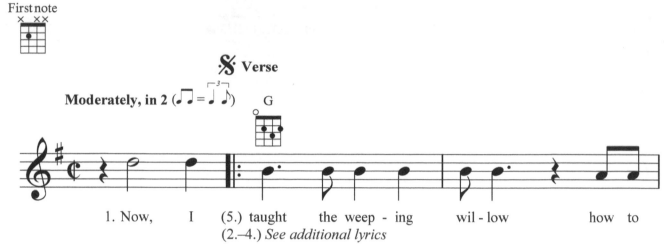

1. Now, I (5.) taught the weep - ing wil - low how to
(2.–4.) *See additional lyrics*

cry, and I showed the clouds how to

cov - er up a clear, blue sky. And the

tears that I cried for that wom - an _____ are gon - na flood you, big

To Coda

riv - er. Then I'm gon - na sit right here un - til I

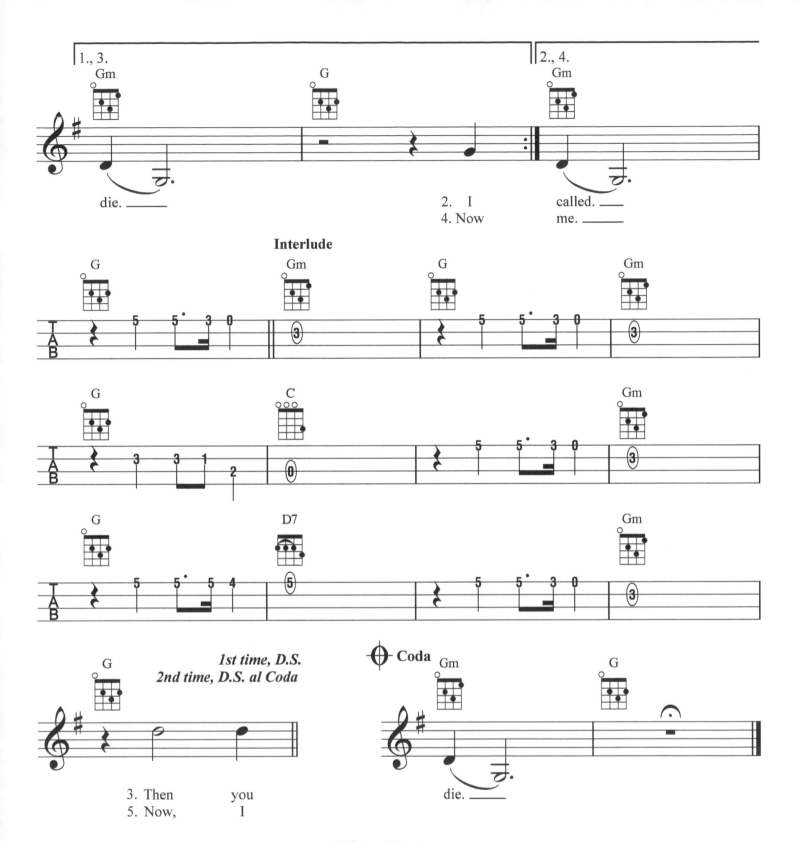

Additional Lyrics

2. I met her accidentally in St. Paul, Minnesota,
   And it tore me up every time I heard her drawl, Southern drawl.
   Then I heard my dream was back downstream, cavortin' in Davenport,
   And I followed you, big river, when you called.

3. Then you took me to St. Louis later on down the river.
   A freighter said she's been here, but she's gone, boy, she's gone.
   I found her trail in Memphis, but she just walked up the block.
   She raised a few eyebrows and then she went on down alone.

4. Now, won't you batter down by Baton Rouge? River Queen, roll it on.
   Take that woman on down to New Orleans, New Orleans.
   Go on, I've had enough; dump my blues down in the Gulf.
   She loves you, big river, more than me.

A Boy Named Sue

Words and Music by Shel Silverstein

First note

Moderately bright

(Spoken:) 1. Well, my daddy left home when I was three and he didn't leave much to
3.–10. See additonal lyrics

Ma and me, just this old guitar and an empty bottle of booze. Now, I don't

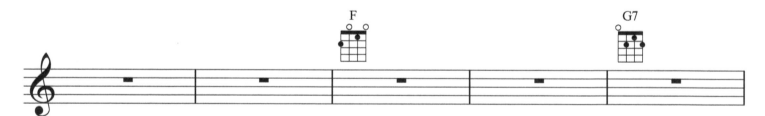

blame him because he run and hid, but the meanest thing that he ever did was, before he left he

went and named me Sue. 2. Well, he must have thought it was

quite a joke, and it got lots of laughs from a lot of folks. It seems I had to

fight   my   whole   life   through.   *Some   gal   would   giggle   and I'd   get red,   and   some*

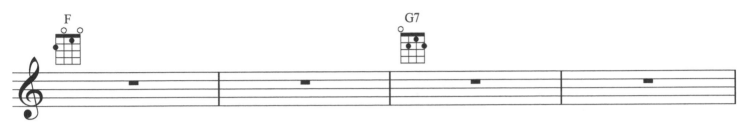

guy would   laugh   and I'd   bust   his   head.   *I   tell   you,   life   ain't   easy   for   a   boy   named*

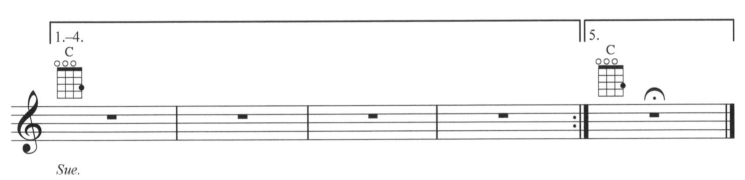

Sue.

Additional Lyrics

3. *Well, I grew up quick and I grew up mean;*
   My fists got hard and my wits got keen.
   Roamed from town to town to hide my shame.
   But I made me a vow to the moon and stars,
   I'd search the honky-tonks and bars,
   And kill that man that give me that awful name.

4. *Well, it was Gatlinburg in mid July,*
   And I had just hit town and my throat was dry.
   I'd thought I'd stop and have myself a brew.
   At an old saloon on a street of mud,
   There at a table dealin' stud,
   Sat the dirty, mangy dog that named me Sue.

5. *Well, I knew that snake was my own sweet dad*
   From a worn-out picture that my mother had.
   And I knew that scar on his cheek and his evil eye.
   He was big and bent and gray and old,
   And I looked at him and my blood ran cold,
   And I said, "My name is Sue. How do you do?
   Now you gonna die." Yeah, that's what I told him.

6. *Well, I hit him hard right between the eyes,*
   And he went down, but to my surprise
   He come up with a knife and cut off a piece of my ear.
   But I busted a chair right across his teeth
   And we crashed through the wall and into the street,
   Kickin' and a-gougin' in the mud and the blood and the beer.

7. *I tell you, I've fought tougher men,*
   But I really can't remember when.
   He kicked like a mule and he bit like a crocodile.
   I heard him laugh and then I heard him cussin',
   He went for his gun and I pulled mine first.
   He stood there lookin' at me and I saw him smile.

8. *And he said, "Son, this world is rough,*
   And if a man's gonna make it, he's gotta be tough.
   And I know I wouldn't be there to help you along.
   So I gave you that name and I said goodbye.
   I knew you'd have to get tough or die.
   And it's that name that helped to make you strong.

9. *Yeah, he said, "Now, you just fought one helluva fight,*
   And I know you hate me and you've got the right
   To kill me now, and I wouldn't blame you if you do.
   But you ought to thank me before I die
   For the gravel in your guts and the spit in your eye,
   'Cause I'm the son of a bitch that named you Sue."
   Yeah, what could I do? What could I do?

10. *I got all choked up and I threw down my gun,*
    Called him my pa and he called me his son.
    And I come away with a different point of view.
    And I think about him now and then,
    Ev'ry time I try and ev'ry time I win.
    And if I ever have a son, I think I'm gonna name him...
    Bill or George. Anything but Sue.
    I still hate that man. Yeah.

Cry, Cry, Cry

Words and Music by John R. Cash

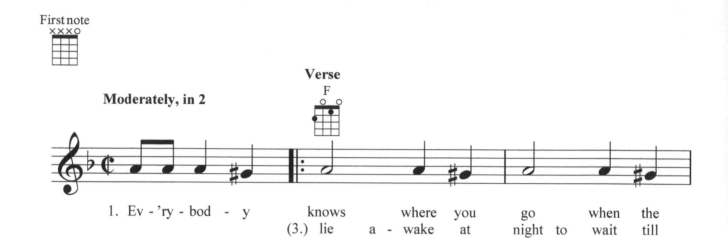

Moderately, in 2

Verse

1. Ev - 'ry - bod - y   knows   where   you   go   when the
(3.) lie   a - wake   at   night   to   wait   till

sun   goes   down.   I   think   you   on - ly   live   to   see   the
you   come   in.   You   stay   a   lit - tle   while   and   then   you're

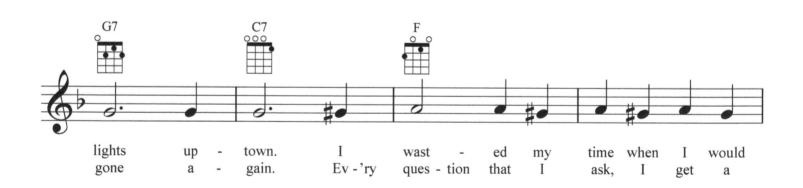

lights   up - town.   I   wast - ed   my   time   when   I   would
gone   a - gain.   Ev - 'ry   ques - tion   that   I   ask,   I   get   a

try,   try,   try,   'cause   when   the   lights   have   lost   their   glow   you'll
lie,   lie,   lie.   For   ev - 'ry   lie   you   tell   you're   gon - na

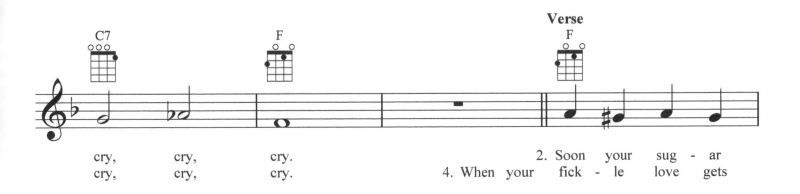

cry,   cry,   cry.
cry,   cry,   cry.

2. Soon your sug - ar
4. When your fick - le love gets

dad - dies   will   all   be   gone.   You'll wake up some
old, no one will care for you.   Then you'll come back to

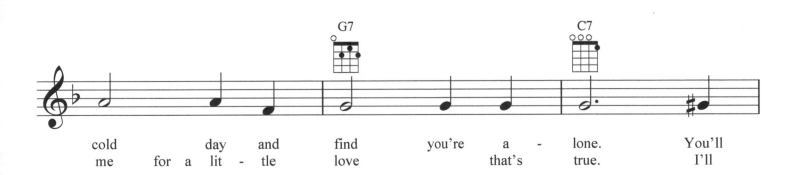

cold   day   and   find   you're   a - lone.   You'll
me   for a lit - tle   love   that's   true.   I'll

call   for   me,   but   I'm gon - na tell   you   bye,   bye,
tell   you   no   and   then you'll ask   me   why,   why,

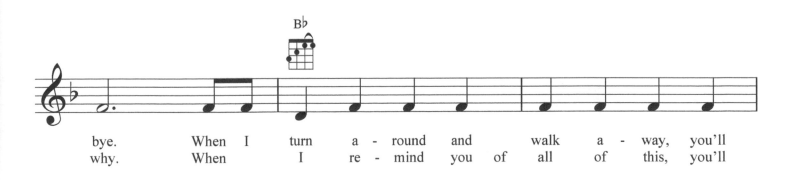

bye.   When I turn a - round and   walk a - way, you'll
why.   When I re - mind you of all of this, you'll

cry,   cry,   cry.
cry,   cry,   cry.   You're gon - na   cry,   cry,

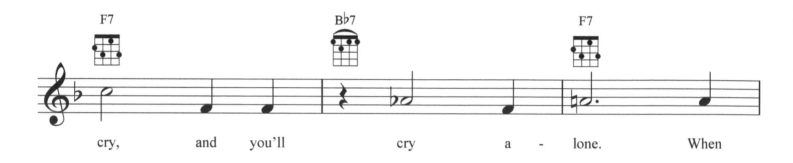

cry,   and you'll   cry   a - lone.   When

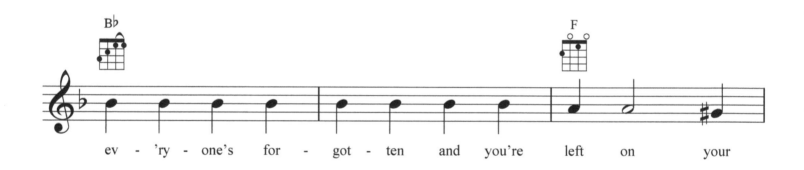

ev - 'ry - one's   for - got - ten   and   you're   left   on   your

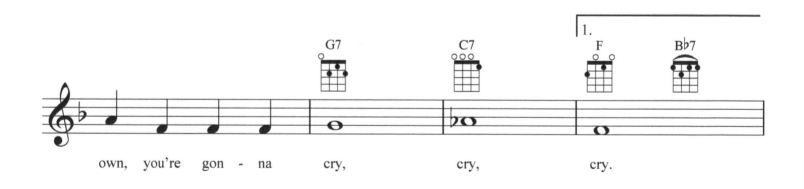

own, you're gon - na   cry,   cry,   cry.

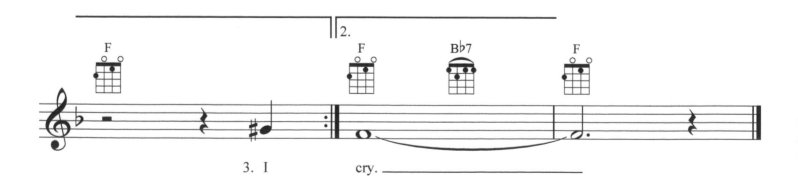

3. I   cry. _____

Daddy Sang Bass

Words and Music by Carl Perkins

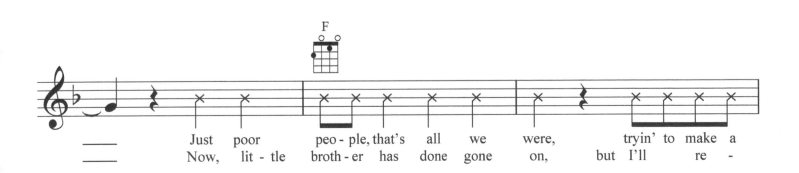

cir - cle, sing - in' loud. _____ ⎫

yon - der in a lit - tle while. _____ ⎬ Dad - dy sang

Chorus

bass, Ma - ma sang ten - or. Me and lit - tle broth - er would join right

in there. Sing - in' seems to help a trou - bled

soul. _____ One of these days, and it won't be

long, I'll re - join them in a song. I'm gon - na

join the fam - 'ly cir - cle at the throne. _____ No, the

Don't Take Your Guns to Town

Words and Music by Johnny R. Cash

First note

Verse
Moderately, in 2

1. A young cow - boy named Bil - ly Joe grew
(2.–5.) *See additional lyrics*

rest - less on the farm. A boy filled with

wan - der - lust, who real - ly meant no harm. He

changed his clothes and shined his boots and combed his dark hair

down, and his moth - er cried as he walked out: "Don't

Chorus

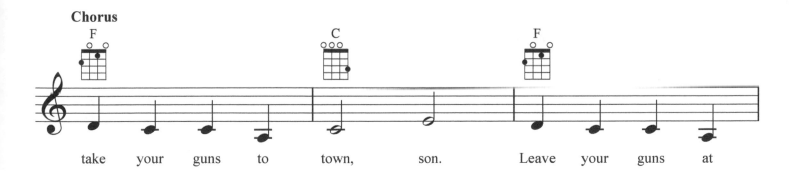

take   your   guns   to   town,   son.   Leave   your   guns   at

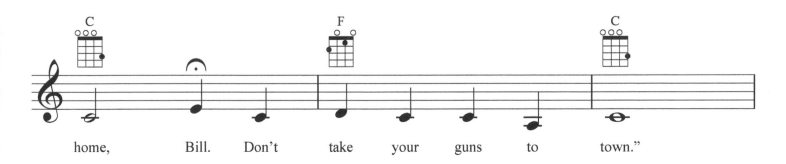

home,   Bill.   Don't   take   your   guns   to   town."

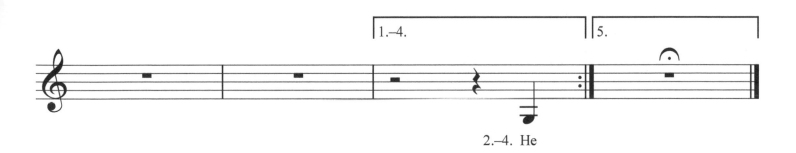

2.–4. He

Additional Lyrics

2. He laughed and kissed his mom and said, "Your Billy Joe's a man.
 I can shoot as quick and straight as anybody can.
 But I wouldn't shoot without a cause; I'd gun nobody down."
 But she cried again as he rode away:

3. He sang a song as on he rode, his guns hung at his hips.
 He rode into a cattle town, a smile upon his lips.
 He stopped and walked into a bar and laid his money down.
 But his mother's words echoed again:

4. He drank his first strong liquor then to calm his shaking hand,
 And tried to tell himself at last he had become a man.
 A dusty cowpoke at his side began to laugh him down,
 And he heard again his mother's words:

5. Filled with rage, then Billy Joe reached for his gun to draw.
 But the stranger drew his gun and fired it before he even saw.
 As Billy Joe fell to the floor the crowd all gathered 'round,
 And wondered at his final words:

Flesh and Blood

Words and Music by John R. Cash

1. Be - side a sing - in' moun - tain stream where the
(2.) leaned a - gainst the bark of a birch and I

pus - sy wil - low grew, where sil - ver leaf of
breathed the hon - ey dew, saw a north - bound

ma - ple spar - kled in the morn - ing
flock of geese a - gainst the sky of

dew, I braid - ed twigs of wil - low, made a
ba - by blue. A - mong the lil - y pads I carved a ____

string of buck - eye beads. But flesh and blood needs
whis - tle from a reed, while hon - ey - suck - le

flesh   and   blood,   and   you   are   what   I
wine   is   sweet,   and   but   you   are   what   I

need.
need.

Flesh   and   blood   needs   flesh   and   blood,   and

1.

you   are   what   I   need. _____   2. I

Verse

2.

3. A   mock - ing - bird   sang   just   for   me   and   I

thanked   him   for   the   song.   Then   dark - ness   float - ed

up   the   hill   and   I   had   to   move   a - long.

Those   are   a   few   lit - tle   things   on   which   the

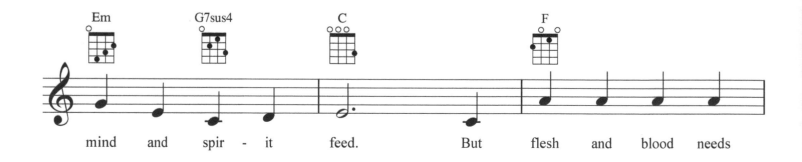

mind   and   spir - it   feed.   But   flesh   and   blood   needs

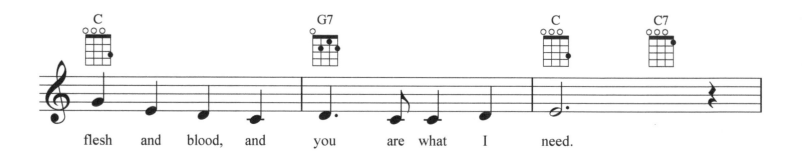

flesh   and   blood,   and   you   are   what   I   need.

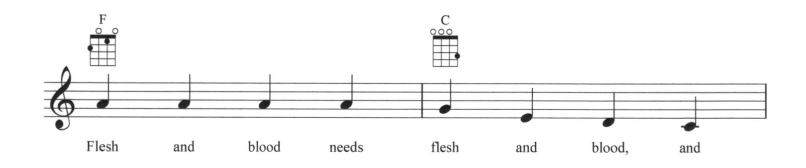

Flesh   and   blood   needs   flesh   and   blood,   and

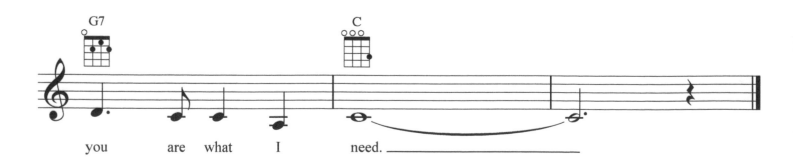

you   are   what   I   need. _____

If I Were a Carpenter

Words and Music by Tim Hardin

First note

Verse
Moderately, in 2

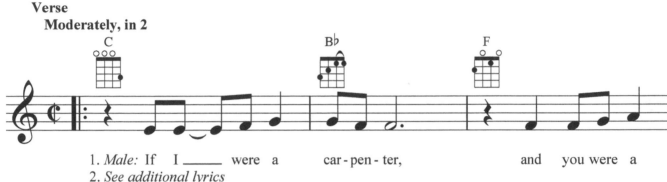

1. *Male:* If I _____ were a car - pen - ter, and you were a
2. *See additional lyrics*

la - dy, would you mar - ry me an - y - way?

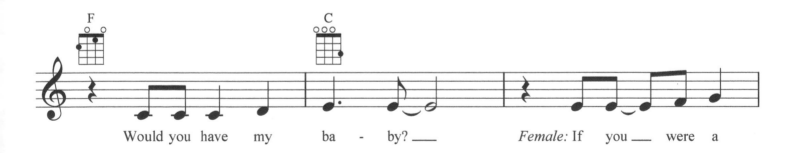

Would you have my ba - by? _____ *Female:* If you _____ were a

car - pen - ter, and I were a la - dy,

I'd mar - ry you an - y - way. I'd have your

ba - by. ___ *Male:* If a tin - ker was my trade, ___

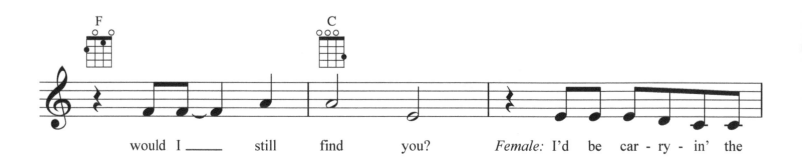

would I ___ still find you? *Female:* I'd be car - ry - in' the

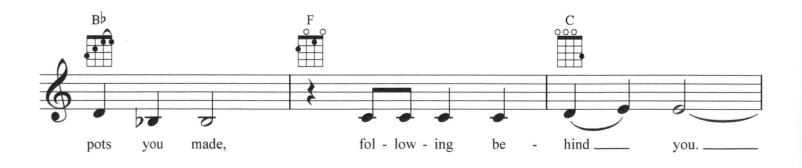

pots you made, fol - low - ing be - hind ___ you. ___

Chorus

___ *Both:* Save your love through lone - li - ness, ___

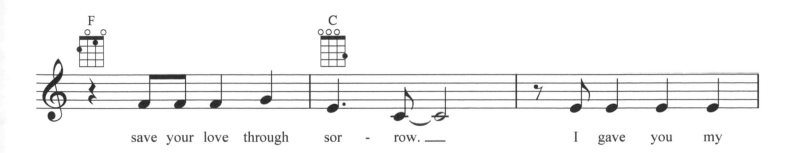

save your love through sor - row. ___ I gave you my

on - li - ness; ___ give me your to - mor - row.

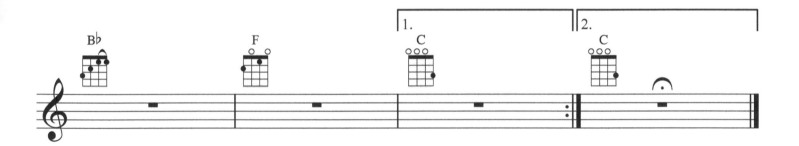

Additional Lyrics

2. *Male:* If I were a miller at a mill wheel grindin',
        Would you miss your colored blouse and your soft shoes shinin'?

Female: If you were a miller at a mill wheel grindin',
        I'd not miss my colored blouse and my soft shoes shinin'.

Male: If I worked my hands in wood, would you still love me?
Female: I'd answer you, "Yes, I would. *Male:* And would you not be above me...

Male: ...If I were a carpenter, and you were a lady?
Female: I'd marry you anyway. I'd have your baby.

Folsom Prison Blues

Words and Music by John R. Cash

First note

Verse
Moderately, in 2

1. I hear the train a-com-in', it's
(2.–4.) *See additional lyrics*

roll-in' 'round the bend, ____ and I ain't seen the sun-

-shine since I don't __ know when. I'm

stuck in Fol-som Pris-on and time keeps

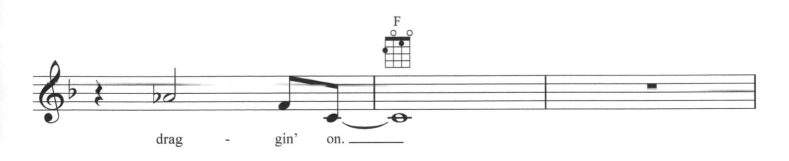

drag - gin' on. _____

But that train keeps a roll -

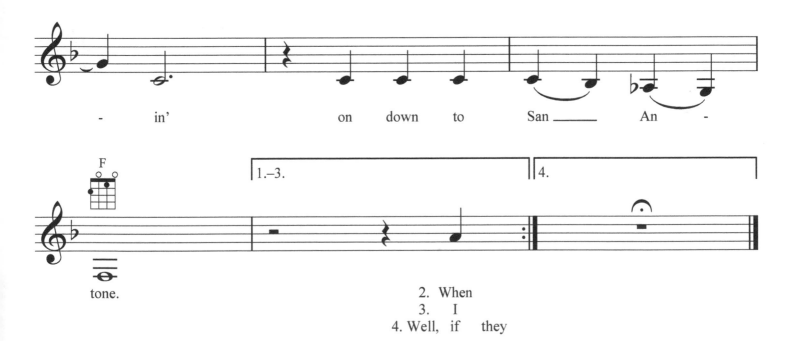

- in'   on   down   to   San _____ An -

1.–3.

4.

tone.

     2. When
     3.   I
   4. Well, if   they

Additional Lyrics

2. When I was just a baby, my mama told me, "Son,
    Always be a good boy; don't ever play with guns."
    But I shot a man in Reno, just to watch him die.
    When I hear that whistle blowin', I hang my head and cry.

3. I bet there's rich folks eatin' in a fancy dining car.
    They're prob'ly drinkin' coffee and smokin' big cigars.
    Well, I know I had it comin', I know I can't be free.
    But those people keep a-movin' and that's what tortures me.

4. Well, if they freed me from this prison, if that railroad train was mine,
    I bet I'd move it on a little farther down the line.
    Far from Folsom Prison, that's where I want to stay,
    And I'd let that lonesome whistle blow my blues away.

(Ghost) Riders in the Sky
(A Cowboy Legend)
By Stan Jones

1. An old cow-poke went rid-ing out one dark and wind-y day.
(2.–4.) See additional lyrics

Up-on a ridge he rest-ed as he went a-long his way,

when all at once a might-y herd of red-eyed cows he saw a-

plow-in' thru the rag-ged skies and up the cloud-y draw.

Chorus

Yi-pi-yi-ay, yi-pi-yi-o,

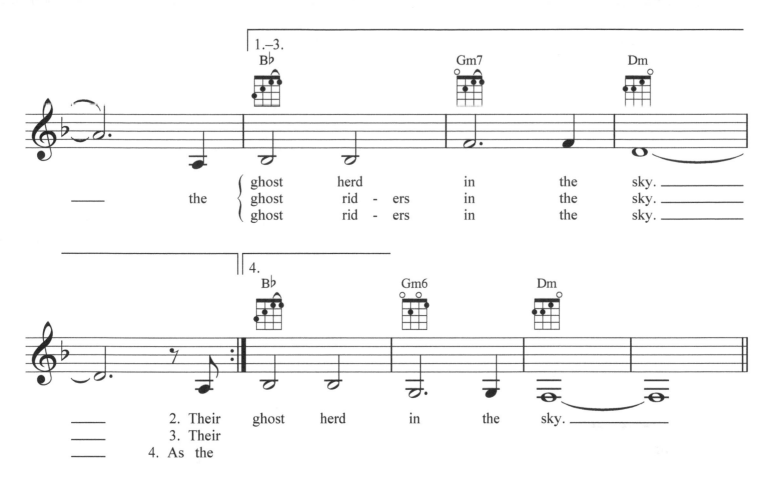

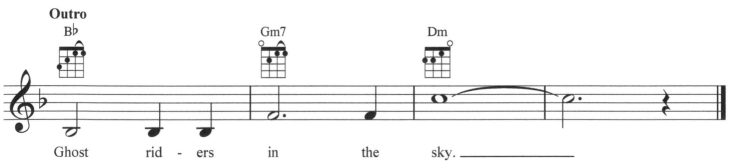

_____ Ghost rid - ers in the sky. _____

Additional Lyrics

2. Their brands were still on fire and their hooves was made of steel.
   Their horns was black and shiny and their hot breath he could feel.
   A bolt of fear went through him as they thundered through the sky,
   For he saw the riders comin' hard as he heard their mournful cry.

3. Their faces gaunt, their eyes were blurred and shirts all soaked with sweat.
   They're ridin' hard to catch that herd, but they ain't caught them yet,
   'Cause they've got to ride forever on that range up in the sky
   On horses snortin' fire; as they ride on, hear their cry.

4. As the riders loped on by him, he heard one call his name.
   "If you want to save your soul from hell a-ridin' on our range,
   Then, cowboy, change your ways today or with us you will ride,
   A-tryin' to catch the devil's herd across these endless skies."

Guess Things Happen That Way

Words and Music by Jack Clement

guess things hap-pen that way. _____

Chorus

God gave me that girl to lean on,

then He put me on my own. __ Heav-en, help me

be a man and have the strength to stand a-lone. __

I don't like it, but I guess things hap-pen that

1.

2.

way.   2. You

Hey, Porter

Words and Music by John R. Cash

First note

Verse
Fast Country, in 2

1. Hey, por - ter, hey, por - ter, would you tell me the time? ___
(2.–5.) *See additional lyrics*

___ How much long - er will it be till we cross ___ that

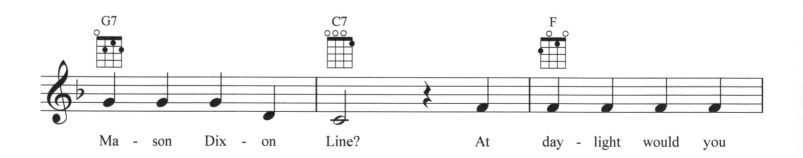

Ma - son Dix - on Line? At day - light would you

tell that en - gi - neer to slow it down? Or

bet - ter   still, __   just   stop   the   train __   'cause   I   wan - na   look   a -

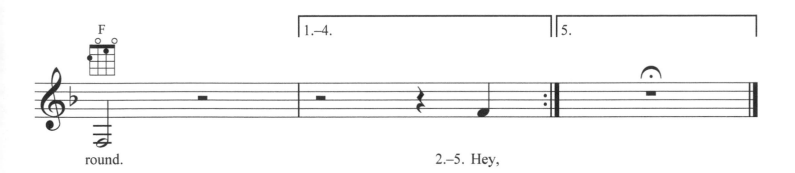

round.   2.–5. Hey,

Additional Lyrics

2. Hey, porter, hey, porter,
   What time did you say?
   How much longer will it be
   Till I can see the light of day?
   When we hit Dixie, would you tell
   That engineer to ring his bell,
   And ask everybody that ain't asleep
   To stand right up and yell?

3. Hey, porter, hey, porter,
   It's gettin' light outside.
   This ol' train is puffin' smoke
   And I have to strain my eyes.
   But ask that engineer if he
   Will blow his whistle, please,
   'Cause I smell frost on cotton leaves
   And I feel that southern breeze.

4. Hey, porter, hey, porter,
   Please get my bags for me.
   I need nobody to tell me now
   That we're in Tennessee.
   Go tell that engineer to make
   That lonesome whistle scream.
   We're not so far from home,
   So take it easy on the steam.

5. Hey, porter, hey, porter,
   Please open up the door.
   When they stop this train, I'm gonna get off first
   'Cause I can't wait no more.
   Tell that engineer I said thanks a lot
   And I didn't mind the fare.
   I'm gonna set my feet on southern soil
   And breathe that southern air.

I Walk the Line

Words and Music by John R. Cash

First note

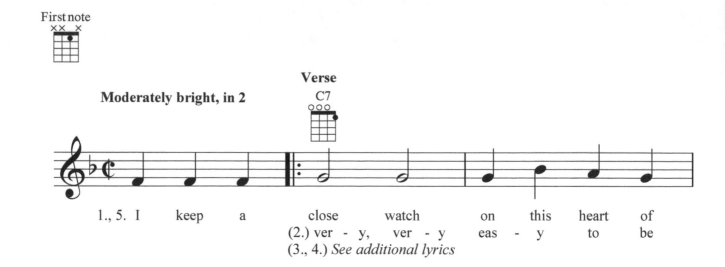

Moderately bright, in 2

Verse

1., 5. I keep a close watch on this heart of
(2.) ver - y, ver - y eas - y to be
(3., 4.) *See additional lyrics*

mine. _____ I keep my eyes wide
true. _____ I find my - self a - lone

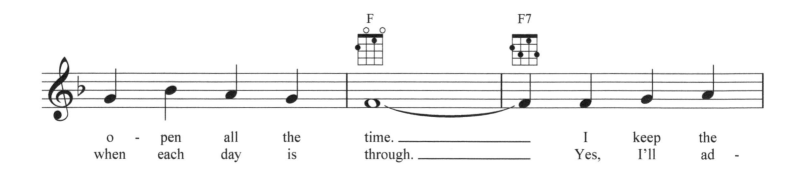

o - pen all the time. _____ I keep the
when each day is through. _____ Yes, I'll ad -

ends out for the tie that binds. _____
mit that I'm a fool for you. _____

Be - cause you're mine, _____ I walk the line. _____

1.–4.
F

5. F

2. I find it line. _____
3. As sure as
4. You've got a

Additional Lyrics

3. As sure as night is dark and day is light,
   I keep you on my mind both day and night.
   And happiness I've known proves that it's right.
   Because you're mine, I walk the line.

4. You've got a way to keep me on your side.
   You give me a cause for love that I can't hide.
   For you I know I'd even try to turn the tide.
   Because you're mine, I walk the line.

Jackson

Words and Music by Billy Edd Wheeler and Jerry Leiber

First note

Verse
Moderately fast

1. We got mar-ried in a fe-ver, hot-ter than a pep-per
(3., 5.) *See additional lyrics*

sprout. We've been talk-in' 'bout Jack-son ev-er since the fire went _

out. _____ I'm goin' to Jack-son, I'm gon-na mess a-

round. _ Yeah, I'm goin' to Jack-son. Look out, Jack-son

town.

Verse

2. Well, go on down to _____ Jack-son.
(4.) *See additional lyrics*

Go a-head and wreck your ___ health. Go play your ___ hand, you ___ big-talk-in' man, and make ___ a big fool of ___ your-self. Yeah, go to

F   C

Jack-son. Go comb your hair. Hon-ey, I'm gon-na snow-ball

F   G   1. C   2. C

Jack-son. See if I care. 3. When fan.

⊕ Coda

D.C. al Coda

C

5. Well, now, ___   back.

Additional Lyrics

3. When I breeze into that city,
   People gonna stoop and bow.
   All them women gonna make me
   Teach 'em what they don't know how.
   I'm goin' to Jackson.
   You turn loose-a my coat,
   'Cause I'm goin' to Jackson.
   "Goodbye," that's all she wrote.

4. But they'll laugh at you in Jackson,
   And I'll be dancin' on a pony keg.
   They'll lead you 'round town like a scolded hound
   With your tail tucked between your legs.
   Yeah, go to Jackson,
   You big-talkin' man.
   And I'll be waitin' in Jackson,
   Behind my Japan fan.

5. Well, now, we got married in a fever,
   Hotter than a pepper sprout.
   We've been talkin' 'bout Jackson
   Ever since the fire went out.
   I'm goin' to Jackson,
   And that's a fact.
   Yeah, we're goin' to Jackson,
   Ain't never comin' back.

Luther's Boogie
(Luther Played the Boogie)

Words and Music by John R. Cash

First note

Verse
Moderately fast, in 2

1. We were just a plain ol' _____ hill - bill - y band ___
(2.) did our best ___ to en - ter - tain ev - 'ry -

___ with a plain ol' coun - try style. We nev - er
where we'd go. We'd

played the kind ___ of songs that would drive an - y - bod - y wild.
near - ly wear ___ our fin - gers off to give the ___ folks a show.

Played a rail - road song ___ with a stomp - in' beat, ___ we played a
Played "Jump - in' Jack" ___ to make 'em get in a groove, ___ we played

blues song kind - a slow and sweet. ___ But the thing that knocked ___ 'em
sad songs real ___ slow and smooth. ___ But the on - ly thing ___ that would

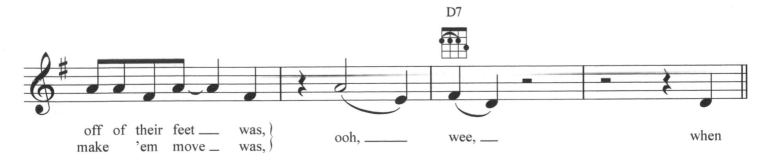

off of their feet ___ was,⟩
make 'em move ___ was,⟩   ooh, _____ wee, ___   when

Chorus

Lu - ther played the boo - gie woo - gie,   Lu - ther played the boo - gie woo - gie,

Lu - ther played the boo - gie woo - gie,   Lu - ther played the boo - gie woo - gie,

Lu - ther played the boo - gie woo - gie,   Lu - ther played the boo - gie woo - gie,

Lu - ther played the boo - gie woo - gie,   Lu - ther played the boo - gie in the

strang - est kind   of _____ way.

Katy Too

Words and Music by John R. Cash and Jack Clement

Mar - y Ann, just tell her I'm her lov - in' man.

Give my love to Jane and Sue, but don't

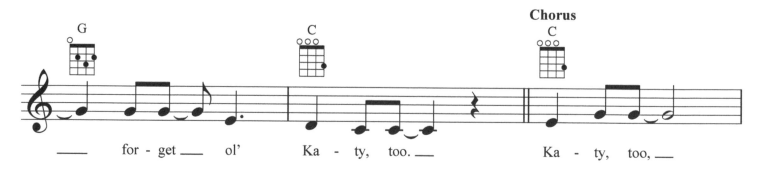

Chorus

for - get ol' Ka - ty, too. Ka - ty, too,

Ka - ty, too, don't for - get ol' Ka - ty, too.

Interlude

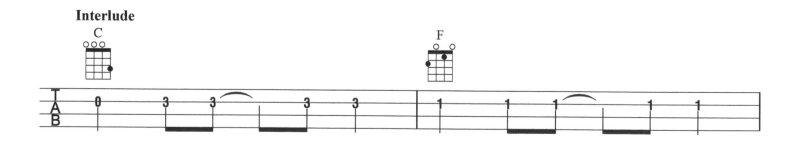

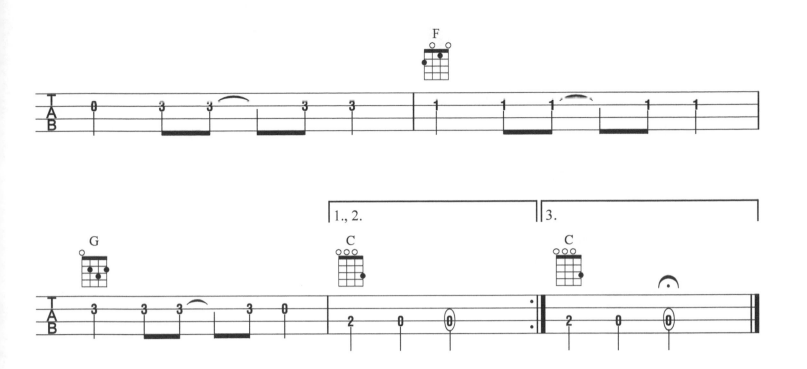

Additional Lyrics

3. I like Sadie's chicken stew and Susie's good at pitchin' woo.
   I like Mary's barbecue, but I still like ol' Katy, too.
Chorus: Katy, too, Katy, too, I still like ol' Katy, too.

4. Now, girls, I'm not the flirty kind, but I just can't make up my mind.
   I'd like to marry all of you, but I still miss ol' Katy, too.
Chorus: Katy, too, Katy, too, I still miss ol' Katy, too.

5. To all the girls, I make this toast. I love you ev'ry one the most.
   But don't ask me to say, "I do," 'cause I still miss ol' Katy, too.
Chorus: Katy, too, Katy, too, I still miss ol' Katy, too.

6. Cupid, you've been good to me; I've got more girls than I can see.
   But if you give me all but two, then let's squeeze in ol' Katy, too.
Chorus: Katy, too, Katy, too, let's squeeze in ol' Katy, too.

The Man in Black

Words and Music by John R. Cash

First note

Verse

Moderately, in 2

1. Well, you won - der why I al - ways dress in
(3.) wear the black for _____ those who nev - er

black, _____ why you nev - er see bright
read _____ or _____ lis - tened to the

col - ors on my back. _____ And
words that Je - sus said _____ a -

why does my ap - pear - ance seem to have a som - ber
bout the road to hap - pi - ness through love and char - i -

tone? Well, there's a rea - son for the things that I have
ty. Why, you'd think He's talk - in' straight to you and

Verse

C

5. wear   it   for   the   sick   and   lone - ly   old, _____
(7.) things   that   nev - er   will   be   right,   I   know, _____

___   for   the   reck - less   ones whose   bad   trip   left   them
___   and ___ things   need   chang - in'   ev - 'ry - where   you

D7   G7   F

cold. _____   I   wear   the   black   in
go. _____   But un - til   we   start   to

Em7   Dm7   G7   C

mourn - in'   for   the   lives   that   could have   been.   Each
make   a   move   to   make   a   few things   right,   you'll

D7

week   we   lose   a   hun - dred   fine   young
nev - er   see   me   wear   a   suit   of

G7   **Verse**
                                       C

men. _____   6. Ah,   I   wear   it   for   the
white. _____   8. Oh,   I'd   love   to   wear   a

thou - sands who have died, _____ be -
rain - bow ev - 'ry day _____ and

D7

liev - in' that the Lord was on their side. _____
tell the world that ev - 'ry - thing's o - kay. _____

G7   F   Em7

___ And I wear it for an - oth - er hun - dred
___ But I'll try to car - ry off a lit - tle

Dm7   G7   C   D7

thou - sand who have died be - liev - in' that we
dark - ness on my back. Till things are bright - er,

1.   G7

all were on their side. _____ 7. Well, there's

2.
G7   C

I'm the man in black. _____

One Piece at a Time

Words and Music by Wayne Kemp

Verse

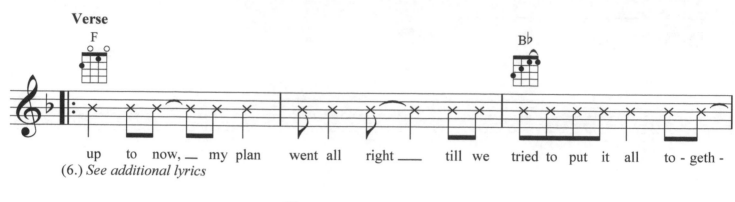

up to now, __ my plan went all right __ till we tried to put it all to-geth-

(6.) *See additional lyrics*

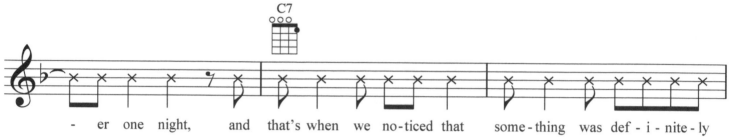

- er one night, and that's when we no-ticed that some-thing was def-i-nite-ly

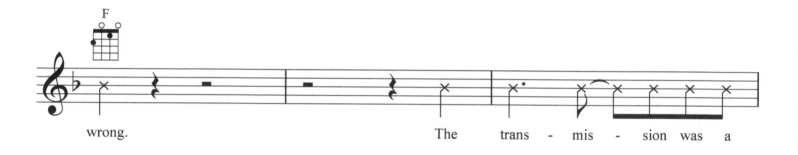

wrong. The trans - mis - sion was a

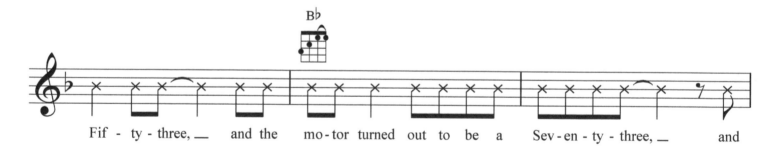

Fif - ty - three, __ and the mo-tor turned out to be a Sev-en-ty-three, __ and

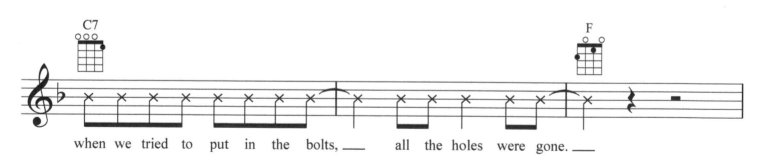

when we tried to put in the bolts, __ all the holes were gone. __

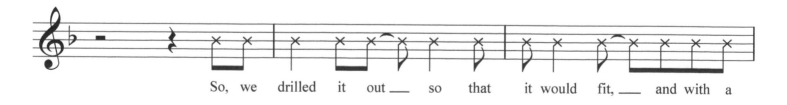

So, we drilled it out __ so that it would fit, __ and with a

little bit of help from an a-dapt-er kit, we had the en-gine run-

-ning just like a song. ___

1.

2. *D.S. al Coda 2 (take 4th ending)*

6. Now, the

7. So, we

Interlude

1.–9.

10.

⊕ **Coda 2**

(Spoken:) See additional lyrics

Well, it's a For-

Outro

-ty-nine, Fif-ty, Fif-ty-one, Fif-ty-two, Fif-ty-three, Fif-ty-four,

Fif-ty-five, Fif-ty-six, Fif-ty-sev-en, Fif-ty-eight, Fif-ty-nine au-to-mo-bile. ___

___ It's a Six-ty, Six-ty-one,

Six - ty - two, Six - ty- three, Six - ty - four, Six - ty - five, Six - ty - six, Six - ty - sev - en,

Six - ty - eight, Six - ty - nine, Sev - en - ty au - to - mo - bile.

Additional Lyrics

2. One day I devised myself a plan
   That should be envy of most any man.
   I'd sneak it out of there in a lunch box in my hand.
   Now, gettin' caught meant gettin' fired,
   But I figured I'd have it all by the time I retired.
   I'd have me a car worth at least a hundred grand.

3. So, the very next day when I punched in
   With my big lunch box and with help from my friend,
   I left that day with a lunch box full of gears.
   I've never considered myself a thief,
   But GM wouldn't miss just one little piece,
   Especially if I strung it out over several years.

4. The first day I got me a fuel pump,
   And the next day I got me an engine and a trunk.
   Then I got me a transmission and all the chrome.
   The little things I could get in my big lunch box
   Like nuts and bolts and all four shocks.
   But the big stuff we snuck out in my buddy's mobile home.

6. Now, the headlights, they was another sight.
   We had two on the left and one on the right.
   But when we pulled out the switch,
       all three of 'em come on.
   The back end looked kinda funny, too.
   But we put it together, and when we got through,
   Well, that's when we noticed that we
       only had one tail fin.
   About that time, my wife walked out,
   And I could see in her eyes that she had her doubts.
   But she opened the door and said,
       "Honey, take me for a spin."

7. So, we drove uptown just to get the tags,
   And I headed her right on down the main drag.
   I could hear everybody laughin' for blocks around.
   But up there at the courthouse, they didn't laugh,
   'Cause to type it up, it took the whole staff.
   And when they got through, the
       title weighed sixty pounds.

Interlude: Ah, yeah, Red Rider, this is the Cottonmouth in the Psychobilly Cadillac. Come on. Hah.
Ah, this is the Cottonmouth, and negatory on the cost of this mo-chine, there, Red Rider.
You might say I went right up to the factory and picked it up; it's cheaper that way.
Ah, what model is it?

Orange Blossom Special

Words and Music by Ervin T. Rouse

First note

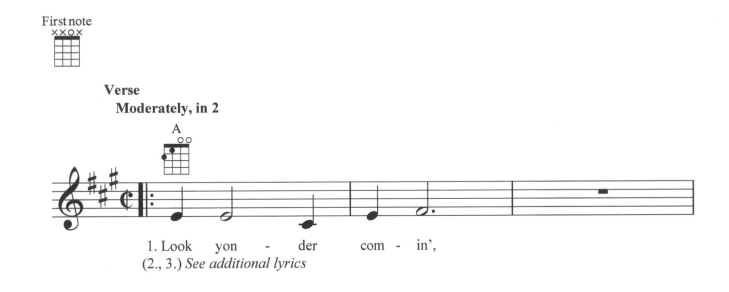

Verse
Moderately, in 2

1. Look yon - der com - in',
(2., 3.) *See additional lyrics*

com - in' down that rail - road track.

Hey, look yon - der com - in',

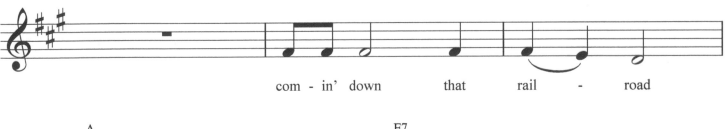

com - in' down that rail - road

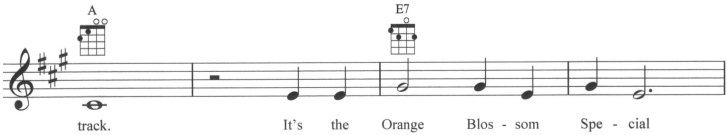

track. It's the Orange Blos - som Spe - cial

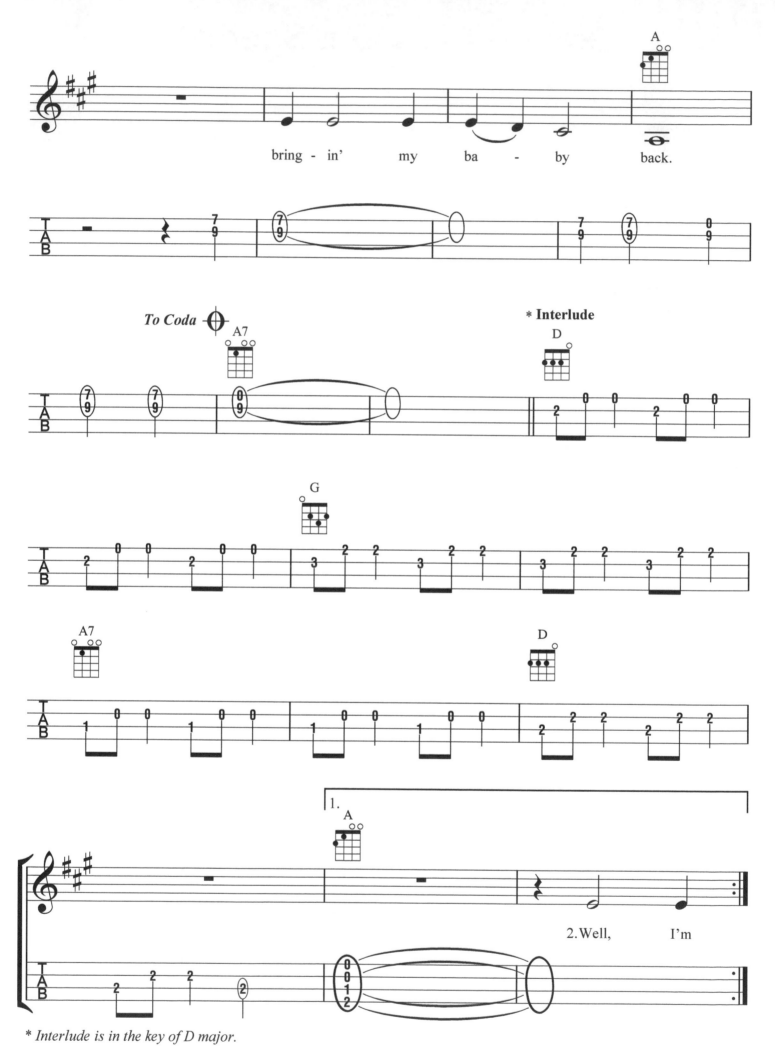

bring - in' my ba - by back.

To Coda ✛ A7

* Interlude

D

G

A7

D

1.
A

2. Well, I'm

* *Interlude is in the key of D major.*

(Spoken): See additional lyrics

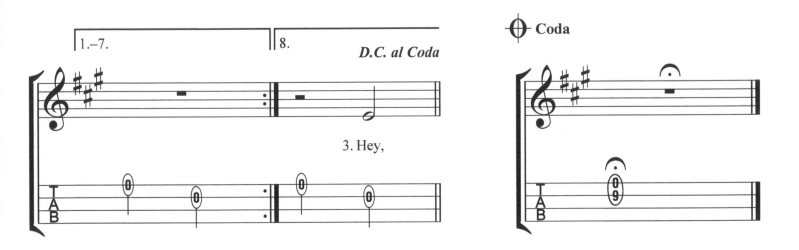

Coda

3. Hey,

Additional Lyrics

2. Well, I'm goin' down to Flor'da and get some sand in my shoes,
   Or maybe Californi' and get some sand in my shoes.
   I'll ride that Orange Blossom Special and lose these New York blues.

Interlude: *Say man, when you goin' back to Florida?*
When am I goin' back to Florida? I don't know. Don't reckon I ever will.
Ain't you worried about gettin' your nourishment in New York?
Uh, I don't care if I do, die, do, die, do, die, do, die, do, die.

3. Hey, talk about a-ramblin', she's the fastest train on the line.
   Talk about a-trav'lin,' she's the fastest train on the line.
   It's that Orange Blossom Special rollin' down the Seaboard Line.

Ring of Fire

Words and Music by Merle Kilgore and June Carter

Additional Lyrics

2. The taste of love is sweet
   When hearts like ours meet.
   I fell for you like a child,
   Oh, but the fire went wild.

Tennessee Flat Top Box

Words and Music by John R. Cash

First note

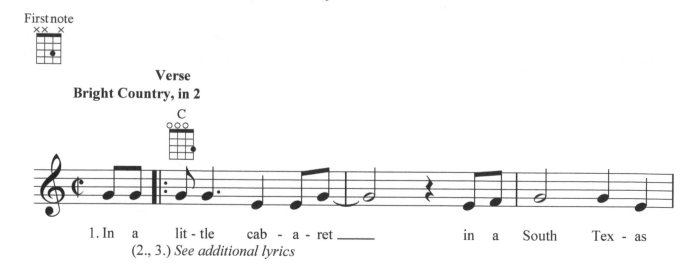

Verse
Bright Country, in 2

1. In a lit-tle cab-a-ret ____ in a South Tex-as
(2., 3.) *See additional lyrics*

bor - der town ____ sat a boy and his gui - tar, ____ and the

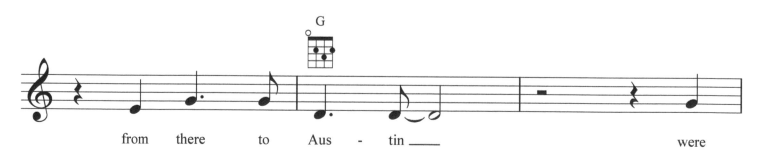

peo - ple came ____ from all a - round. ____ And all the girls ____

from there to Aus - tin ____ were

slip-ping a - way ____ from home and put - ting jewel - ry in hock ____

C
to take a trip
to go and
G
lis - ten
to the lit - tle dark - haired
boy who played the Ten - nes - see flat top
C
box. And he would
Interlude
F
play...
C
F

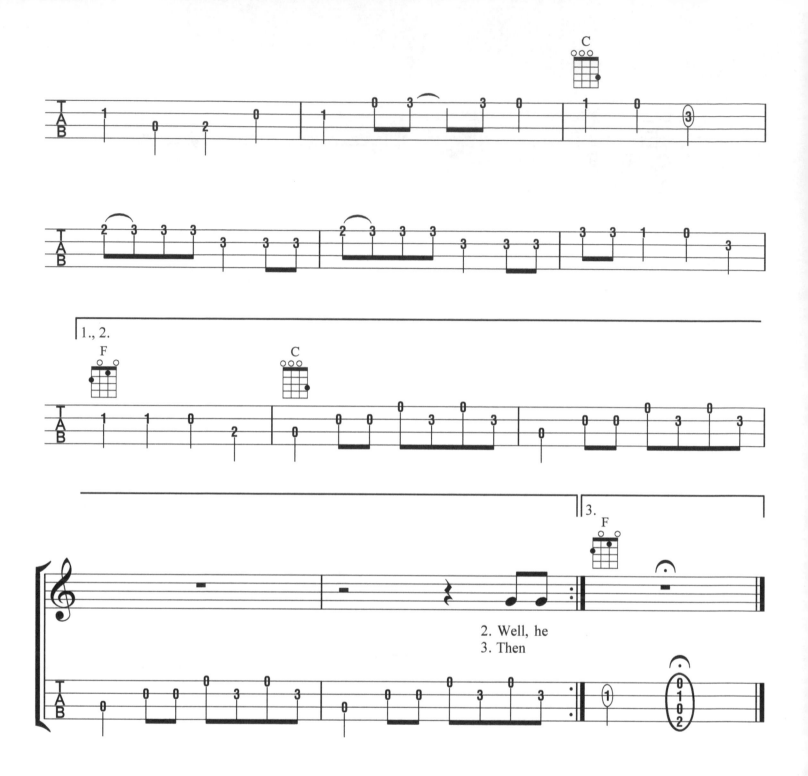

Additional Lyrics

2. Well, he couldn't ride or wrangle,
   And he never cared to make a dime.
   But give him his guitar
   And he'd be happy all the time.
   And all the girls from nine to ninety
   Were snapping fingers, tapping toes
   And begging him, "Don't stop,"
   And hypnotized, and fascinated
   By the little dark-haired boy
   Who played the Tennessee flat top box.
   And he would play...

3. Then one day he was gone,
   And no one ever saw him 'round.
   He vanished like the breeze.
   They forgot him in the little town,
   But all the girls still dreamed about him
   And hung around the cabaret
   Until the doors were locked.
   And then one day on the hit parade
   Was a little dark-haired boy
   Who played the Tennessee flat top box.
   And he would play...

Sunday Mornin' Comin' Down

Words and Music by Kris Kristofferson

First note

Verse
Moderately, in 2

1. Well, I woke up Sun - day morn - in' with no

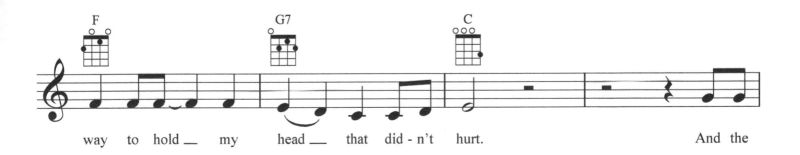

way to hold __ my head __ that did - n't hurt. And the

beer I had __ for break - fast was - n't bad, so I had one more for des -

sert. Then I fum - bled in my clos - et, through my

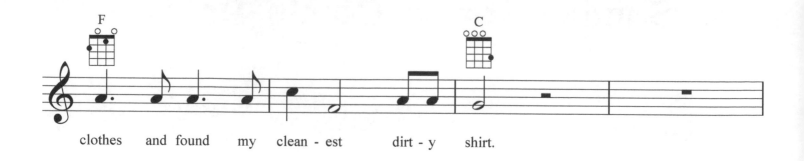

clothes and found my clean - est dirt - y shirt.

Then I washed my face ___ and combed my hair, ___

and stum-bled down the stairs ___ to meet the day. 2. I'd

Verse

smoked my mind ___ the night be - fore ___ with cig - a - rettes and
(3.) *See additional lyrics*

songs ___ I'd been pick - in'.

But I lit my first ___ and watched a small ___ kid

play - in' ___ with a can ___ that he was kick - in'.

Then I walked a - cross ___ the

street ___ and caught the Sun - day smell ___ of some - one's ___

fry - in' chick - en. And, Lord, it

took me back ___ to some - thin' that I lost some - where, ___

some - how a - long the way. On a

Chorus

Sun - day morn - in' side - walk, I'm wish - in', Lord, __

__ that I was stoned. 'Cause there's

some - thin' in a Sun - day that makes a

bod - y feel a - lone. And there's

noth - in' short of dy - in'

that's   half   as   lone - some   as   the   sound

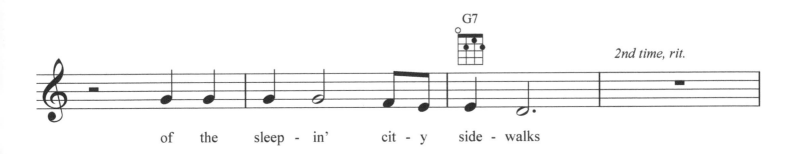

of   the   sleep - in'   cit - y   side - walks

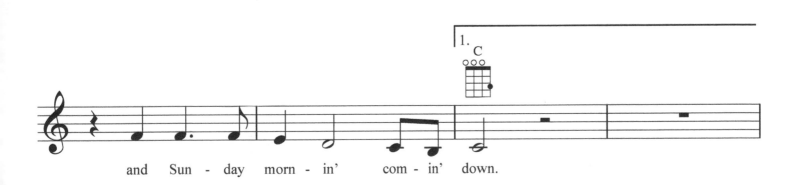

and   Sun - day   morn - in'   com - in'   down.

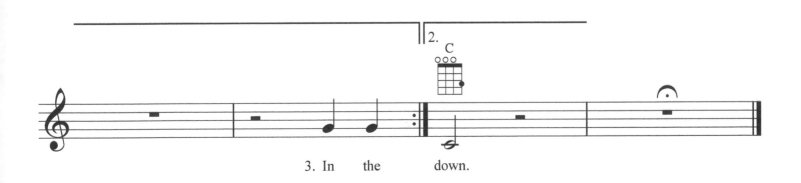

3. In   the   down.

Additional Lyrics

3. In the park I saw a daddy with a laughin' little girl that he was swingin',
   And I stopped beside a Sunday school and listened to the songs they were singin'.
   Then I headed down the streets, and somewhere far away a lonely bell was ringin',
   And it echoed through the canyons like the disappearing dreams of yesterday.

There You Go

Words and Music by John R. Cash

Understand Your Man

Words and Music by John R. Cash

What Is Truth?

Words and Music by John R. Cash

(Spoken:) 1. The old man turned off the radio, said, "Where did all the old songs go? Kids sure play funny music these days. They play it in the strangest ways." Said, "It looks to me like they've all gone wild. It was peaceful back when I was a child."

(Spoken:) 2. The young girl dancin' to the latest beat has found new ways to move her feet. A young man speaking in the city square is trying to tell somebody that he cares. Yeah, the ones that you're callin' wild are gonna be the leaders in a little while. This

Well, man, could it be that the girls and the boys

are tryin' to be heard above your noise? And the

Chorus

lone - ly voice of youth cries, "What is truth?" _____

Verse

_____

(Spoken:) 3. A little boy of three
(Spoken:) 4. A young man sittin' on

sittin' on the floor looks up and says,
the witness stand, the man with the Book

"Daddy, what is war?" "Son, that's when people fight and die."
says, "Raise your hand. Repeat after me: I solemnly swear."

A little boy of three says, "Daddy, why?" A young man of seventeen
The man looked down at his long hair, and although the young

F

in   Sunday   school,   bein'   taught   the   Golden
man   solemnly   swore,   nobody   seemed   to   hear

D7

Rule.   And   by   the   time   another   year   has   gone   around,   it   may
anymore.   And   it   didn't   really   matter   if   the   truth   was   there;   it   was

G7

be   his   turn   to   lay   his   life   down.   Can   you
the   cut   of   his   clothes   and   the   length   of   his   hair.   And   the

C   F   Dm7   G7   C

blame   the   voice   of   youth   for   ask - in',   ⎱
lone - ly   voice   of   youth   cries,   ⎰   "What   is   truth?" _____

G   F   A   G7

C

1.   2.   ***D.C. al Coda***

old world wakened to a newborn day. And I

sol - emn - ly swear that it - 'll be that way.

You'd bet - ter help that voice of youth find

what is truth. And the

Outro

lone - ly voice of youth cries,

"What is truth?" _____